**VOL. 90**

T0101730

## CONTENTS

ISBN 978-1-4234-5197-6

7777 W. BLUEMOUND RD. P.O. BOX 13819 MILWAUKEE, WI 53213

For all works contained herein:
Unauthorized copying, arranging, adapting, recording, Internet posting, public performance,
or other distribution of the printed or recorded music in this publication is an infringement of copyright.
Infringers are liable under the law.

Visit Hal Leonard Online at
**www.halleonard.com**

# Anji

## Words and Music by Davy Graham

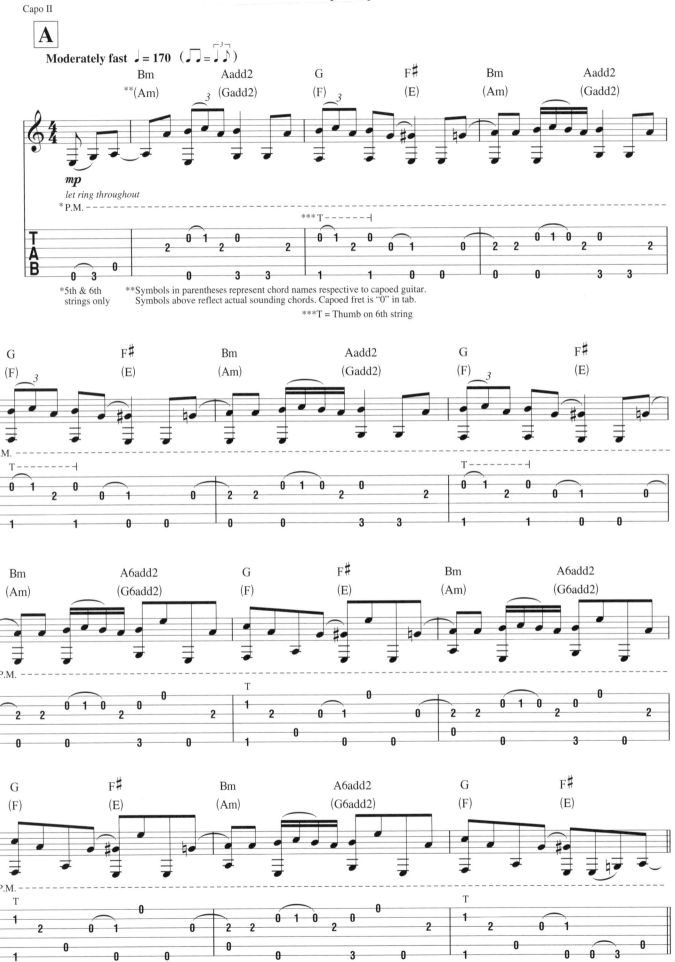

*5th & 6th strings only

**Symbols in parentheses represent chord names respective to capoed guitar. Symbols above reflect actual sounding chords. Capoed fret is "0" in tab.

***T = Thumb on 6th string

© 1965 (Renewed 1993) EMI ROBBINS MUSIC LTD.
All Rights in the U.S. and Canada Controlled and Administered by GLENWOOD MUSIC CORP.
All Rights Reserved   International Copyright Secured   Used by Permission

*Slap strings w/ right hand fingers.

# Cavatina

from the Universal Pictures and EMI Films Presentation THE DEER HUNTER
By Stanley Myers

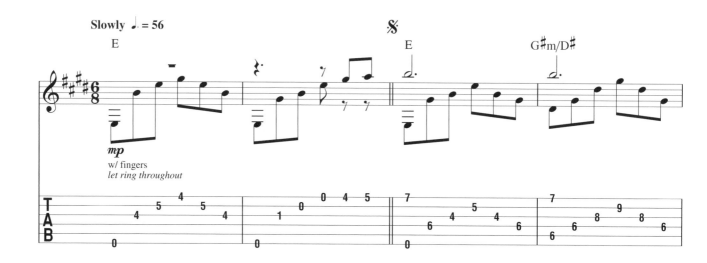

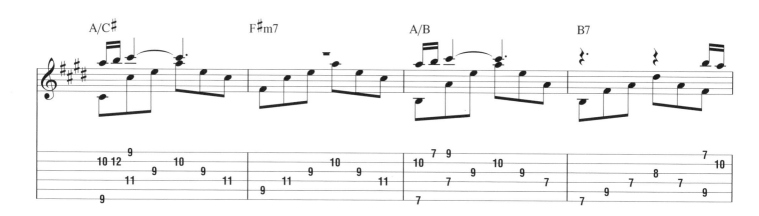

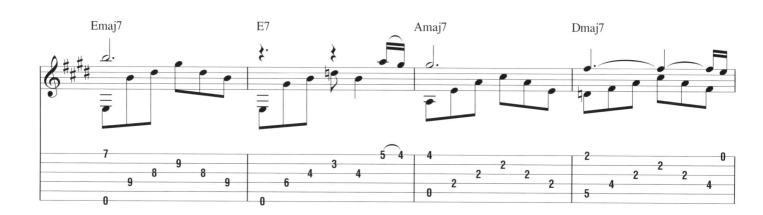

Copyright © 1971, 1979 A.E. Copyrights Ltd.
Copyright Renewed
All Rights for the United States and Canada Controlled by Chrysalis Music
All Rights Reserved   Used by Permission

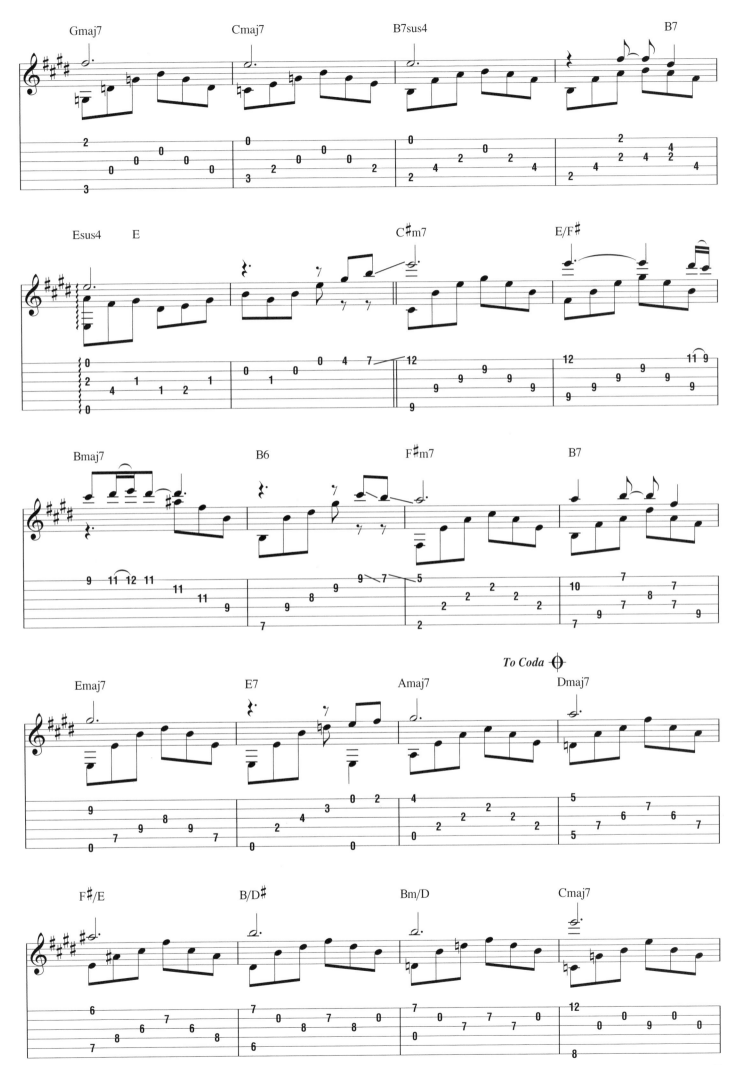

**Coda**

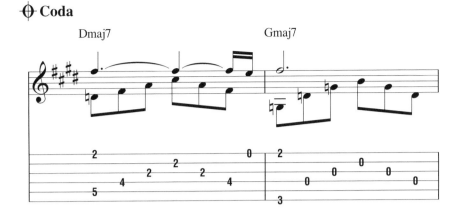

# Classical Gas

**By Mason Williams**

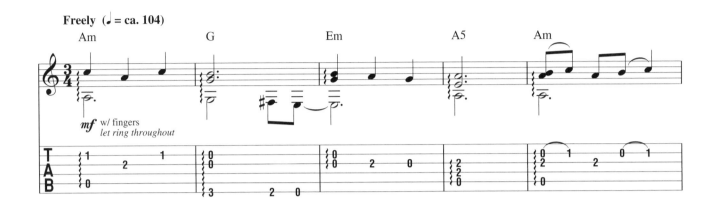

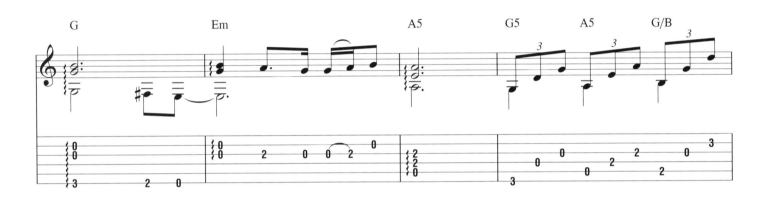

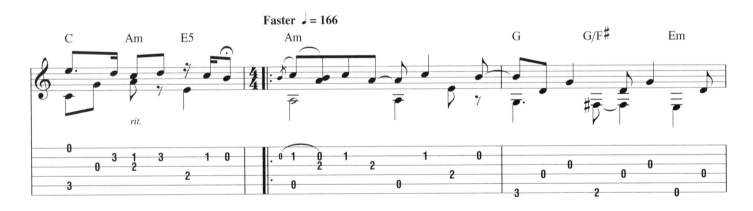

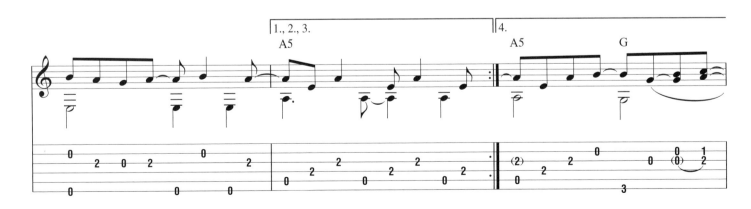

© 1967, 1968 Weems Music Co.
© Renewed 1995, 1996 Weems Music Co.
All Rights Reserved   Used by Permission

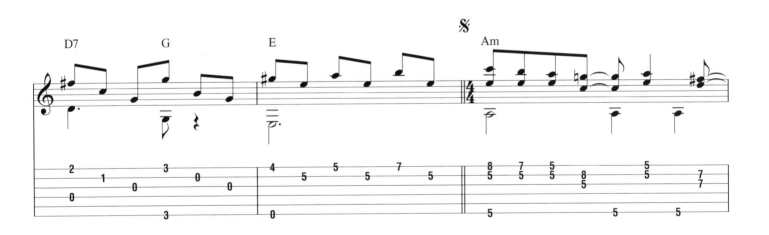

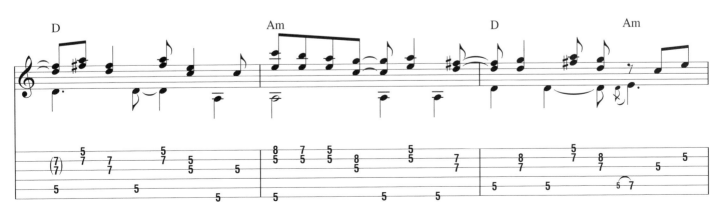

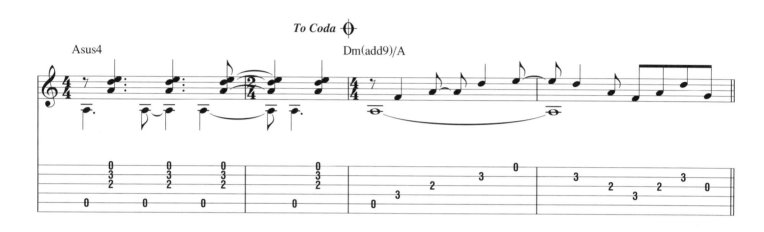

**Coda**

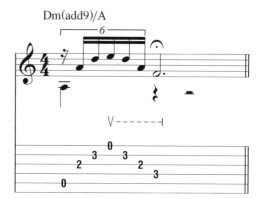

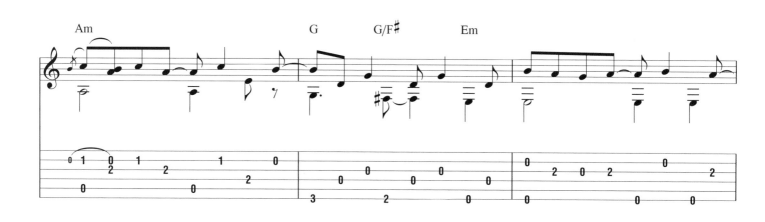

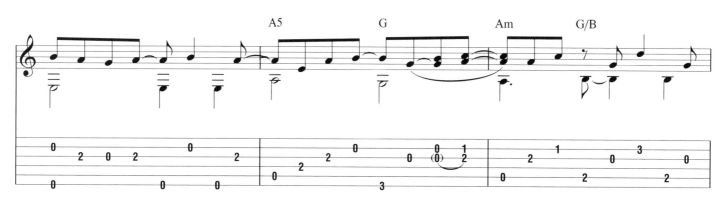

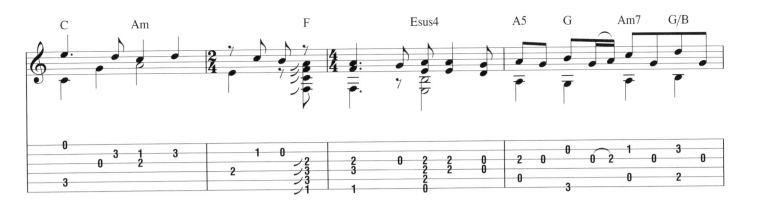

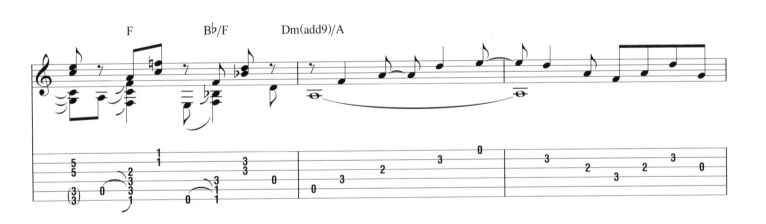

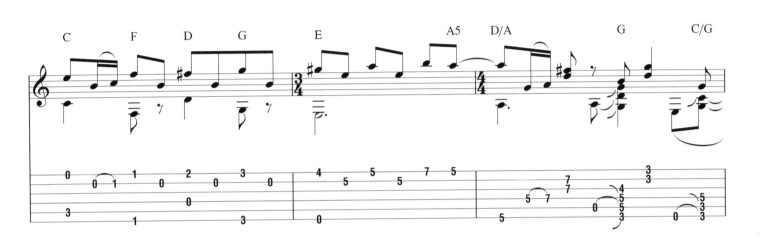

17

# Dee

**Music by Randy Rhoads**

**Slowly** ♩. = 45

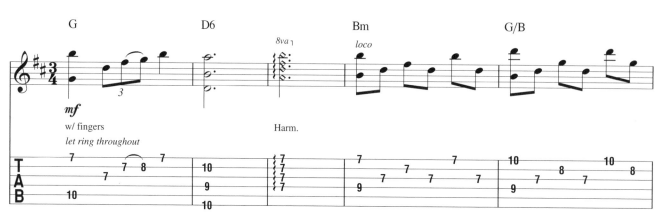

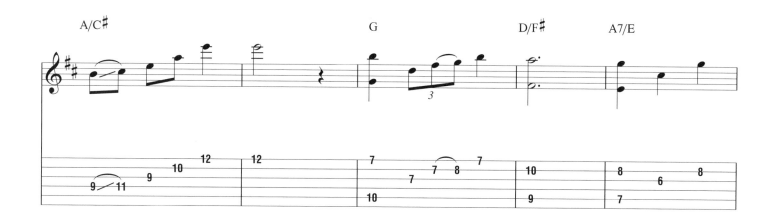

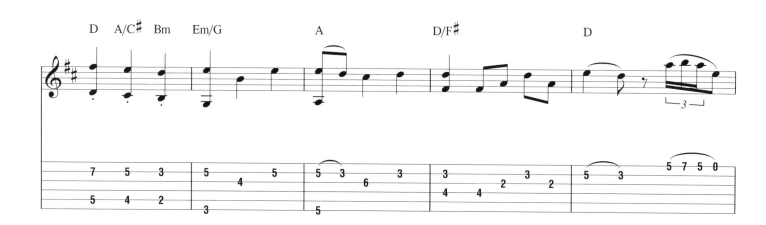

TRO - © Copyright 1981 and 1985 Essex Music International, Inc., New York, NY
International Copyright Secured
All Rights Reserved Including Public Performance For Profit
Used by Permission

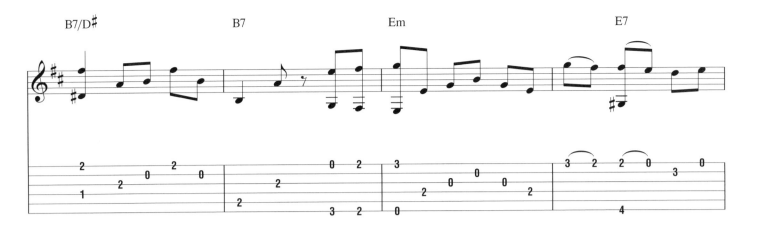

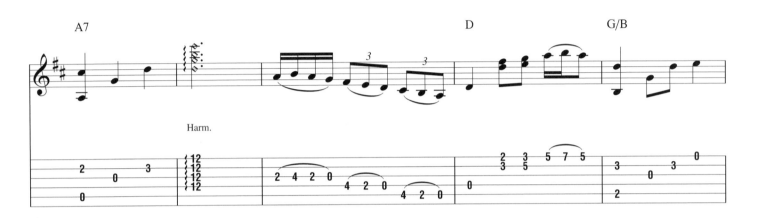

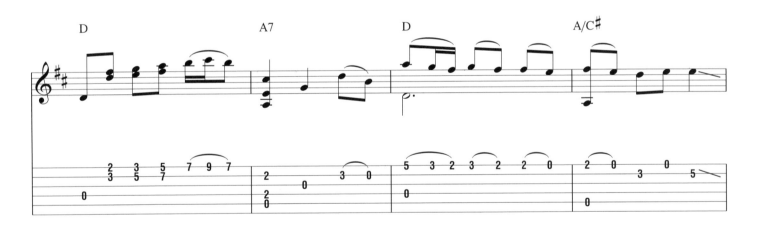

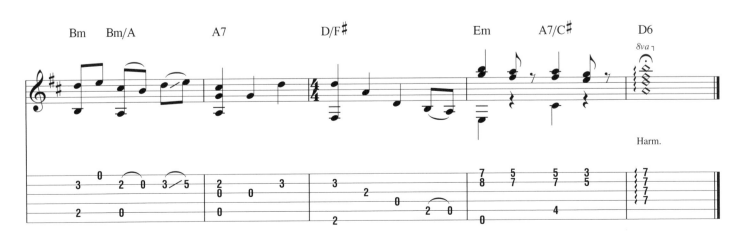

# Embryonic Journey

## By Jorma Kaukonen

Drop D tuning:
(low to high) D-A-D-G-B-E

**Moderately** ♩ = 108

© 1967 (Renewed) Icebag Corp. (BMI)
All Rights Reserved   Used by Permission

# Jesu, Joy of Man's Desiring

**Written by Johann Sebastian Bach**
**Arranged by Leo Kottke**

Open G tuning, down 1/2 step:
(low to high) D♭-G♭-D♭-G♭-B♭-D♭

**Slowly** ♩. = 66

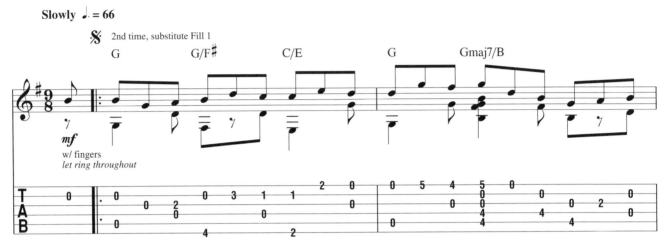

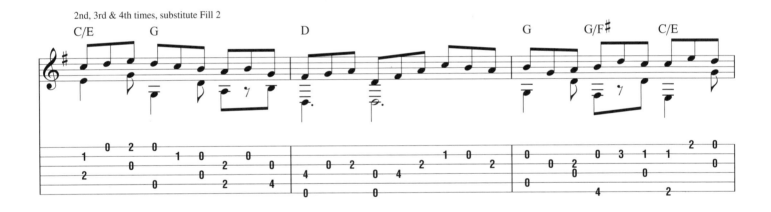

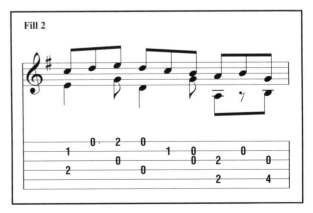

© 1971 (Renewed 1999) OVERDRIVE MUSIC (ASCAP)/Administered by BUG MUSIC
All Rights Reserved   Used by Permission

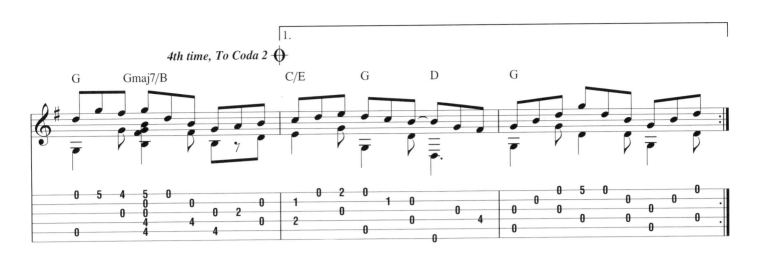

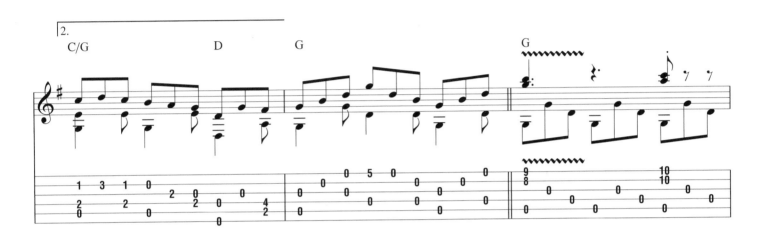

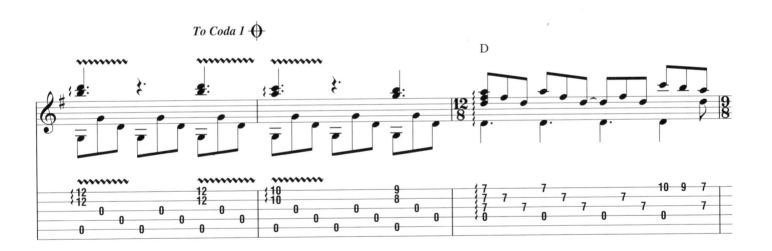

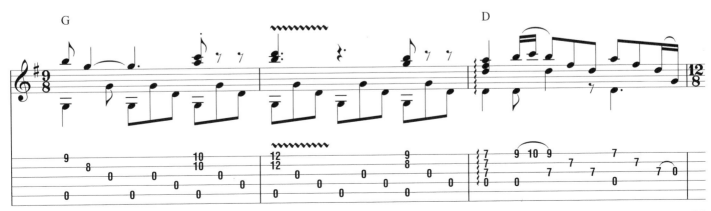

*D.S. al Coda 1*
*(take 2nd ending)*

**Coda 1**

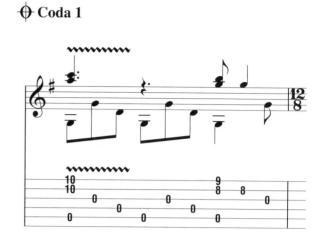

*D.S. al Coda 2*

**Coda 2**

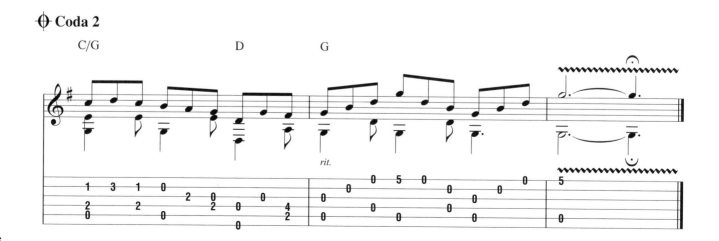

# Malagueña

from the Spanish Suite ANDALUCIA

**Music and Spanish Lyric by Ernesto Lecuona**
**English Lyric by Marian Banks**

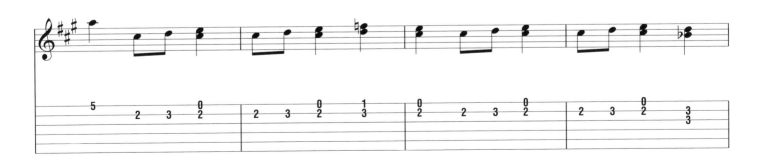

Copyright © 1928 by Edward B. Marks Music Company
Copyright Renewed
International Copyright Secured   All Rights Reserved
Used by Permission

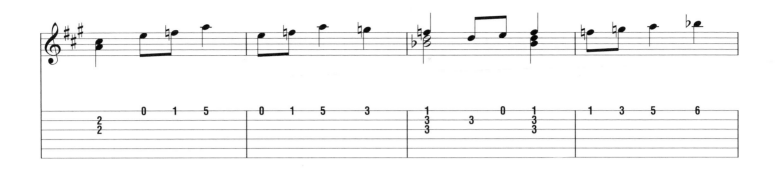

**Slower**

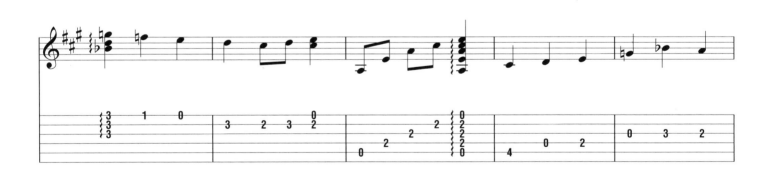

**A tempo**

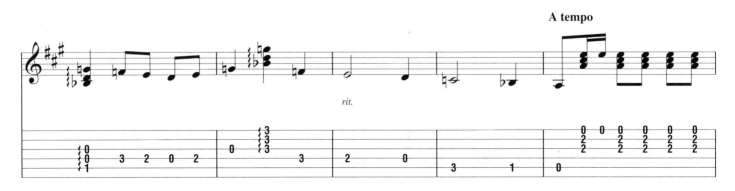

*rit.*

**Freely**

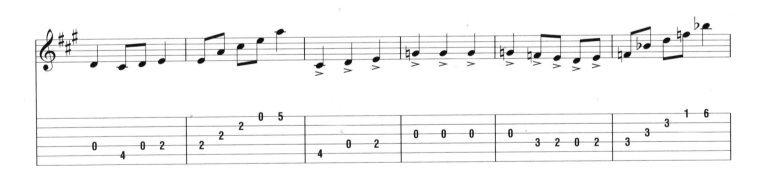

**Free time** *(à la cadenza)*

*rit.*

A tempo

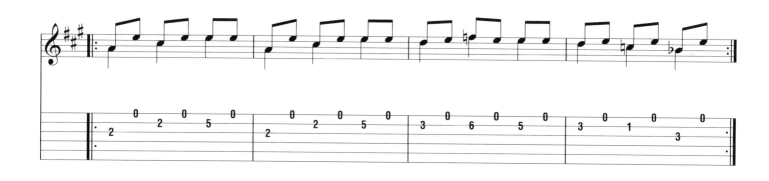

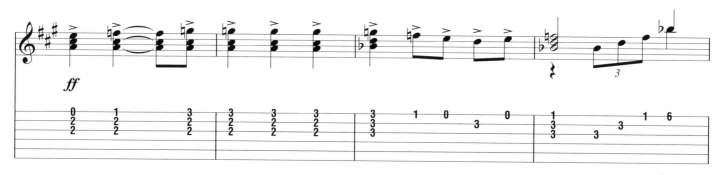

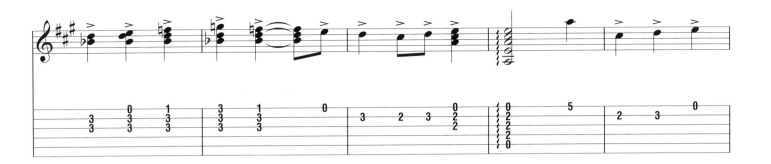

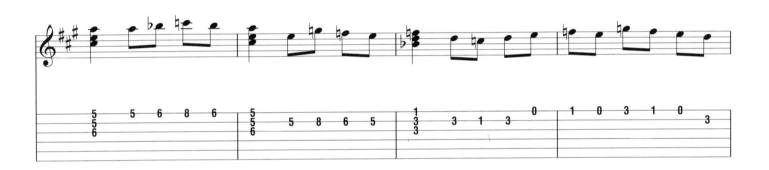

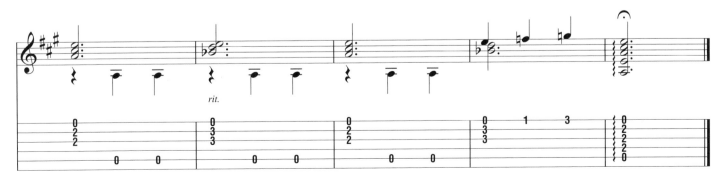

# Spanish Caravan

### Words and Music by The Doors

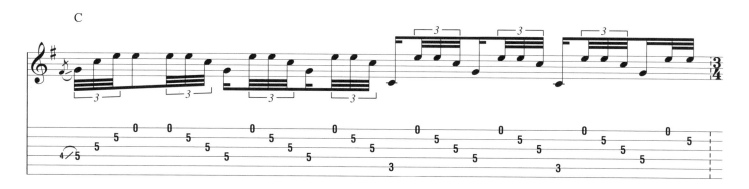

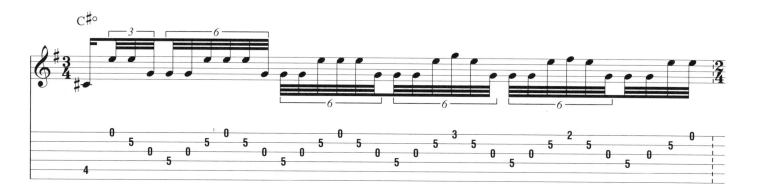

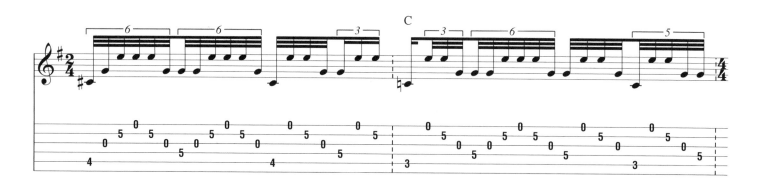

Copyright © 1968 Doors Music Co.
Copyright Renewed
All Rights Reserved   Used by Permission

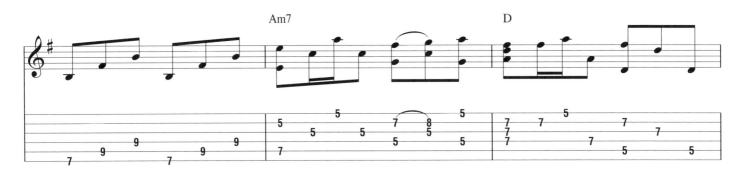

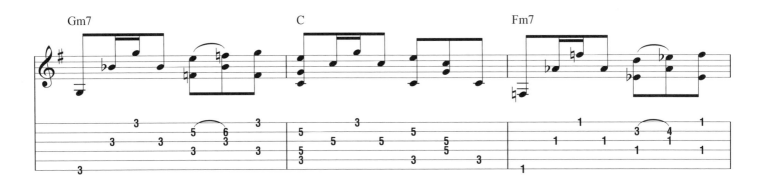

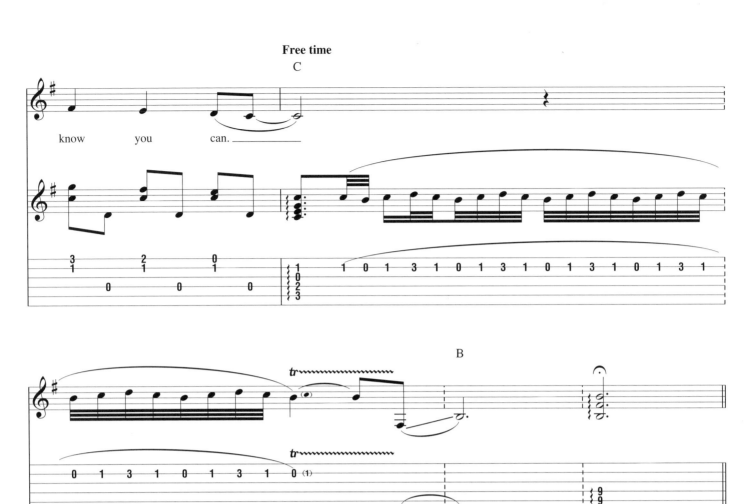

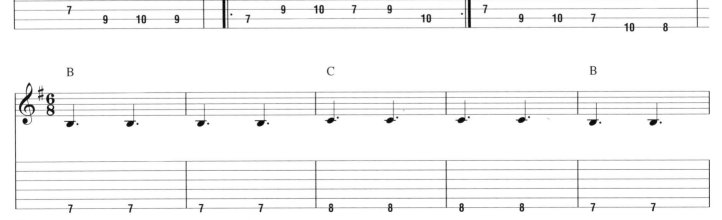

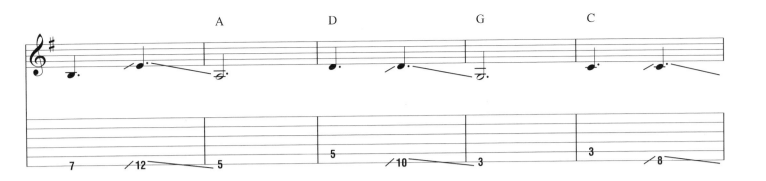

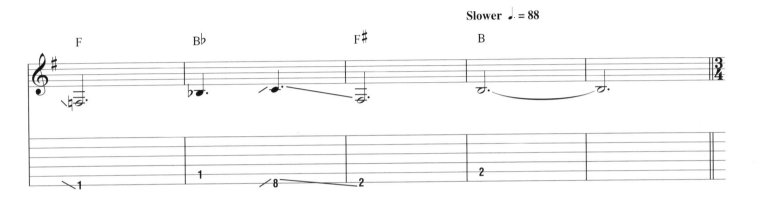

**Slower** ♩. = 88

**Verse**

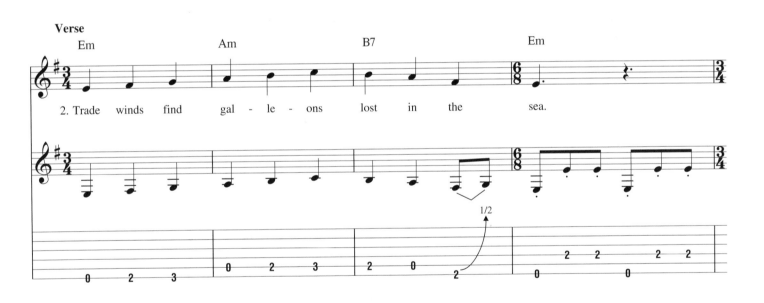

2. Trade winds find gal - le - ons lost in the sea.

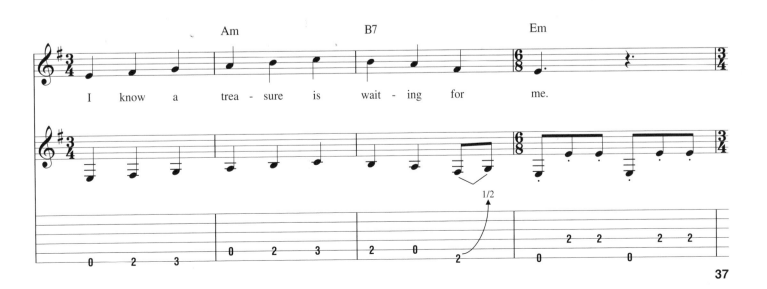

I know a trea - sure is wait - ing for me.

**Outro-Chorus**

**Free time**

# GUITAR NOTATION LEGEND

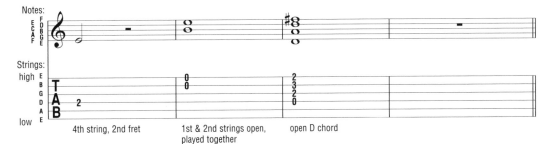

**THE MUSICAL STAFF** shows pitches and rhythms and is divided by bar lines into measures. Pitches are named after the first seven letters of the alphabet.

**TABLATURE** graphically represents the guitar fingerboard. Each horizontal line represents a string, and each number represents a fret.

4th string, 2nd fret

1st & 2nd strings open, played together

open D chord

---

**HALF-STEP BEND:** Strike the note and bend up 1/2 step.

**WHOLE-STEP BEND:** Strike the note and bend up one step.

**GRACE NOTE BEND:** Strike the note and immediately bend up as indicated.

**SLIGHT (MICROTONE) BEND:** Strike the note and bend up 1/4 step.

---

**BEND AND RELEASE:** Strike the note and bend up as indicated, then release back to the original note. Only the first note is struck.

**PRE-BEND:** Bend the note as indicated, then strike it.

**VIBRATO:** The string is vibrated by rapidly bending and releasing the note with the fretting hand.

**PALM MUTING:** The note is partially muted by the pick hand lightly touching the string(s) just before the bridge.

---

**HAMMER-ON:** Strike the first (lower) note with one finger, then sound the higher note (on the same string) with another finger by fretting it without picking.

**PULL-OFF:** Place both fingers on the notes to be sounded. Strike the first note and without picking, pull the finger off to sound the second (lower) note.

**LEGATO SLIDE:** Strike the first note and then slide the same fret-hand finger up or down to the second note. The second note is not struck.

**SHIFT SLIDE:** Same as legato slide, except the second note is struck.

---

**TRILL:** Very rapidly alternate between the notes indicated by continuously hammering on and pulling off.

**TAPPING:** Hammer ("tap") the fret indicated with the pick-hand index or middle finger and pull off to the note fretted by the fret hand.

**NATURAL HARMONIC:** Strike the note while the fret-hand lightly touches the string directly over the fret indicated.

**PINCH HARMONIC:** The note is fretted normally and a harmonic is produced by adding the edge of the thumb or the tip of the index finger of the pick hand to the normal pick attack.

---

**TREMOLO PICKING:** The note is picked as rapidly and continuously as possible.

**VIBRATO BAR DIVE AND RETURN:** The pitch of the note or chord is dropped a specified number of steps (in rhythm), then returned to the original pitch.

**VIBRATO BAR SCOOP:** Depress the bar just before striking the note, then quickly release the bar.

**VIBRATO BAR DIP:** Strike the note and then immediately drop a specified number of steps, then release back to the original pitch.

---

## Additional Musical Definitions

 *(accent)*  •  Accentuate note (play it louder).

 *(staccato)*  •  Play the note short.

**D.S. al Coda**  •  Go back to the sign (𝄋), then play until the measure marked "*To Coda*," then skip to the section labelled "**Coda**."

**D.C. al Fine**  •  Go back to the beginning of the song and play until the measure marked "*Fine*" (end).

**Fill**  •  Label used to identify a brief melodic figure which is to be inserted into the arrangement.

**N.C.**  •  Harmony is implied.

  •  Repeat measures between signs.

  •  When a repeated section has different endings, play the first ending only the first time and the second ending only the second time.

# HAL•LEONARD GUITAR PLAY-ALONG®

This series will help you play your favorite songs quickly and easily. Just  follow the tab and listen to the CD to hear how the guitar should sound, and then play along using the separate backing tracks. Mac or PC users can also slow down the tempo without changing pitch by using the CD in their computer. The melody and lyrics are included in the book so that you can sing or simply follow along.

| | | |
|---|---|---|
| VOL. 1 – ROCK | 00699570 / $16.99 | |
| VOL. 2 – ACOUSTIC | 00699569 / $16.95 | |
| VOL. 3 – HARD ROCK | 00699573 / $16.95 | |
| VOL. 4 – POP/ROCK | 00699571 / $16.99 | |
| VOL. 5 – MODERN ROCK | 00699574 / $16.99 | |
| VOL. 6 – '90s ROCK | 00699572 / $16.99 | |
| VOL. 7 – BLUES | 00699575 / $16.95 | |
| VOL. 8 – ROCK | 00699585 / $12.95 | |
| VOL. 9 – PUNK ROCK | 00699576 / $14.95 | |
| VOL. 10 – ACOUSTIC | 00699586 / $16.95 | |
| VOL. 11 – EARLY ROCK | 00699579 / $14.95 | |
| VOL. 12 – POP/ROCK | 00699587 / $14.95 | |
| VOL. 13 – FOLK ROCK | 00699581 / $14.95 | |
| VOL. 14 – BLUES ROCK | 00699582 / $16.95 | |
| VOL. 15 – R&B | 00699583 / $14.95 | |
| VOL. 16 – JAZZ | 00699584 / $15.95 | |
| VOL. 17 – COUNTRY | 00699588 / $15.95 | |
| VOL. 18 – ACOUSTIC ROCK | 00699577 / $15.95 | |
| VOL. 19 – SOUL | 00699578 / $14.95 | |
| VOL. 20 – ROCKABILLY | 00699580 / $14.95 | |
| VOL. 21 – YULETIDE | 00699602 / $14.95 | |
| VOL. 22 – CHRISTMAS | 00699600 / $15.95 | |
| VOL. 23 – SURF | 00699635 / $14.95 | |
| VOL. 24 – ERIC CLAPTON | 00699649 / $16.95 | |
| VOL. 25 – LENNON & McCARTNEY | 00699642 / $14.95 | |
| VOL. 26 – ELVIS PRESLEY | 00699643 / $14.95 | |
| VOL. 27 – DAVID LEE ROTH | 00699645 / $16.95 | |
| VOL. 28 – GREG KOCH | 00699646 / $14.95 | |
| VOL. 29 – BOB SEGER | 00699647 / $14.95 | |
| VOL. 30 – KISS | 00699644 / $16.99 | |
| VOL. 31 – CHRISTMAS HITS | 00699652 / $14.95 | |
| VOL. 32 – THE OFFSPRING | 00699653 / $14.95 | |
| VOL. 33 – ACOUSTIC CLASSICS | 00699656 / $16.95 | |
| VOL. 34 – CLASSIC ROCK | 00699658 / $16.95 | |
| VOL. 35 – HAIR METAL | 00699660 / $16.95 | |
| VOL. 36 – SOUTHERN ROCK | 00699661 / $16.95 | |
| VOL. 37 – ACOUSTIC METAL | 00699662 / $16.95 | |
| VOL. 38 – BLUES | 00699663 / $16.95 | |
| VOL. 39 – '80s METAL | 00699664 / $16.99 | |
| VOL. 40 – INCUBUS | 00699668 / $17.95 | |
| VOL. 41 – ERIC CLAPTON | 00699669 / $16.95 | |
| VOL. 42 – CHART HITS | 00699670 / $16.95 | |
| VOL. 43 – LYNYRD SKYNYRD | 00699681 / $17.95 | |

| | | |
|---|---|---|
| VOL. 44 – JAZZ | 00699689 / $14.95 | |
| VOL. 45 – TV THEMES | 00699718 / $14.95 | |
| VOL. 46 – MAINSTREAM ROCK | 00699722 / $16.95 | |
| VOL. 47 – HENDRIX SMASH HITS | 00699723 / $19.95 | |
| VOL. 48 – AEROSMITH CLASSICS | 00699724 / $16.99 | |
| VOL. 49 – STEVIE RAY VAUGHAN | 00699725 / $16.95 | |
| VOL. 50 – NÜ METAL | 00699726 / $14.95 | |
| VOL. 51 – ALTERNATIVE '90s | 00699727 / $12.95 | |
| VOL. 52 – FUNK | 00699728 / $14.95 | |
| VOL. 53 – DISCO | 00699729 / $14.99 | |
| VOL. 54 – HEAVY METAL | 00699730 / $14.95 | |
| VOL. 55 – POP METAL | 00699731 / $14.95 | |
| VOL. 56 – FOO FIGHTERS | 00699749 / $14.95 | |
| VOL. 57 – SYSTEM OF A DOWN | 00699751 / $14.95 | |
| VOL. 58 – BLINK-182 | 00699772 / $14.95 | |
| VOL. 59 – GODSMACK | 00699773 / $14.95 | |
| VOL. 60 – 3 DOORS DOWN | 00699774 / $14.95 | |
| VOL. 61 – SLIPKNOT | 00699775 / $14.95 | |
| VOL. 62 – CHRISTMAS CAROLS | 00699798 / $12.95 | |
| VOL. 63 – CREEDENCE CLEARWATER REVIVAL | 00699802 / $16.99 | |
| VOL. 64 – THE ULTIMATE OZZY OSBOURNE | 00699803 / $16.99 | |
| VOL. 65 – THE DOORS | 00699806 / $16.99 | |
| VOL. 66 – THE ROLLING STONES | 00699807 / $16.95 | |
| VOL. 67 – BLACK SABBATH | 00699808 / $16.99 | |
| VOL. 68 – PINK FLOYD – DARK SIDE OF THE MOON | 00699809 / $16.99 | |
| VOL. 69 – ACOUSTIC FAVORITES | 00699810 / $14.95 | |
| VOL. 70 – OZZY OSBOURNE | 00699805 / $16.99 | |
| VOL. 71 – CHRISTIAN ROCK | 00699824 / $14.95 | |
| VOL. 72 – ACOUSTIC '90S | 00699827 / $14.95 | |
| VOL. 73 – BLUESY ROCK | 00699829 / $16.99 | |
| VOL. 74 – PAUL BALOCHE | 00699831 / $14.95 | |
| VOL. 75 – TOM PETTY | 00699882 / $16.99 | |
| VOL. 76 – COUNTRY HITS | 00699884 / $14.95 | |
| VOL. 78 – NIRVANA | 00700132 / $14.95 | |
| VOL. 80 – ACOUSTIC ANTHOLOGY | 00700175 / $19.95 | |
| VOL. 81 – ROCK ANTHOLOGY | 00700176 / $22.99 | |

| | | |
|---|---|---|
| VOL. 82 – EASY SONGS | 00700177 / $12.99 | |
| VOL. 83 – THREE CHORD SONGS | 00700178 / $14.99 | |
| VOL. 84 – STEELY DAN | 00700200 / $16.99 | |
| VOL. 85 – THE POLICE | 00700269 / $16.99 | |
| VOL. 86 – BOSTON | 00700465 / $16.99 | |
| VOL. 87 – ACOUSTIC WOMEN | 00700763 / $14.99 | |
| VOL. 88 – GRUNGE | 00700467 / $16.99 | |
| VOL. 91 – BLUES INSTRUMENTALS | 00700505 / $14.99 | |
| VOL. 92 – EARLY ROCK INSTRUMENTALS | 00700506 / $12.99 | |
| VOL. 93 – ROCK INSTRUMENTALS | 00700507 / $14.99 | |
| VOL. 96 – THIRD DAY | 00700560 / $14.95 | |
| VOL. 97 – ROCK BAND | 00700703 / $14.99 | |
| VOL. 98 – ROCK BAND | 00700704 / $14.95 | |
| VOL. 99 – ZZ TOP | 00700762 / $14.99 | |
| VOL. 100 – B.B. KING | 00700466 / $14.99 | |
| VOL. 102 – CLASSIC PUNK | 00700769 / $14.99 | |
| VOL. 103 – SWITCHFOOT | 00700773 / $16.99 | |
| VOL. 104 – DUANE ALLMAN | 00700846 / $16.99 | |
| VOL. 106 – WEEZER | 00700958 / $14.99 | |
| VOL. 108 – THE WHO | 00701053 / $14.99 | |
| VOL. 109 – STEVE MILLER | 00701054 / $14.99 | |
| VOL. 111 – JOHN MELLENCAMP | 00701056 / $14.99 | |
| VOL. 113 – JIM CROCE | 00701058 / $14.99 | |
| VOL. 114 – BON JOVI | 00701060 / $14.99 | |
| VOL. 115 – JOHNNY CASH | 00701070 / $14.99 | |
| VOL. 116 – THE VENTURES | 00701124 / $14.99 | |
| VOL. 119 – AC/DC CLASSICS | 00701356 / $14.99 | |
| VOL. 120 – PROGRESSIVE ROCK | 00701457 / $14.99 | |
| VOL. 123 – LENNON & MCCARTNEY ACOUSTIC | 00701614 / $16.99 | |

**Complete song lists available online.**

*Prices, contents, and availability subject to change without notice.*

FOR MORE INFORMATION, SEE YOUR LOCAL MUSIC DEALER, OR WRITE TO:

# HAL•LEONARD® CORPORATION
7777 W. BLUEMOUND RD. P.O. BOX 13819 MILWAUKEE, WI 53213

Visit Hal Leonard online at www.halleonard.com